The You Are What You Are Cookbook

Edited by Rachel Loosmore

BGC addresses the challenges faced by adults with learning disabilities. It offers both work experience and education while allowing individual development and confidence building. The project and the way it operates is unique. The decisions effecting the project's development are made by the adults with learning disabilities and the staff's role is to ensure they are achieved.

Adults with learning difficulties suffer problems of discrimination in every walk of life. The lack of opportunities open to them means they are not able to develop in areas they want to. The needs of the group are often neglected. It is obvious that they need to have the same opportunities as all members of society, but sadly this is not so.

Published by Accent Press Ltd - 2005
www.accentpress.co.uk

Designed by Rachel Loosmore, Accent Press Ltd.

Printed and bound in Slovenia by Compass Press Ltd.

All profits from the sale of this book will be donated to BGC
Reg. Charity No. 1091271
Kingsway House, 13 Kingsway, Bedford, MK42 9BJ
www.bedsgardencarers.org.uk

Acknowledgments

With thanks to all the celebrities and their associates, who took the time to send their favourite recipes. Thanks to Tim Branson, whose idea this project was, for his determination. To Jayne Darrington for her patience and to Paul Sutherland for his hard work and persistance. Gratitude also to the team at Accent Press for their willingness to take on this project. Our thanks to you for buying this book because we would not be able to do half of the things that we do at the moment if it were not for projects such as BGC. The funds raised by the sale of this book will help enormously.

Contents

Starters

SANDWICH

Italian ciabatta bread
Rub fresh tomato on it
Little salt
Very little olive oil
Two, but two, drops of Aceto Balsamico
Carpaccio beef
Slices of parmesan cheese over the carpaccio

José Careras — Tenor

COCKLES

Ingredients

¼ pt fresh cockles
2 slices wholemeal bread
butter
freshly ground pepper

Method

Butter bread, place cockles on one piece, sprinkle with pepper.
Cover with the other piece, open mouth, shove in, clamp teeth down on
bread and masticate.

CORNFLAKES (breakfast dish)

Ingredients

cornflakes
milk

Method

Buy a packet of cornflakes.
Open the cardboard box.
Open the sort of plastic packet inside the box.
Pour the contents (sort of yellowy brownish bits of things) into a bowl.
Buy a bottle of milk.
Take the top off the thin end of the bottle.
Invert the bottle gently over the cornflakes, making sure that the milk does not go over the edge of the bowl.

It's very simple to make and absolutely delicious.
An alternative is to use Coca-Cola instead of milk.
Add basil as required.

John Cleese — Comedian and Actor

CRAB QUICHE

Ingredients

Pie crust
½ cup chilled butter
3 tbsp vegetable shortening
2 cups all purpose flour
5-6 tbsp cold water
½ tsp salt

Custard
1½ cups heavy cream
3 eggs + 1 yolk
salt & pepper to taste

Filling
1lb jumbo lump cleaned crabmeat
(fresh not frozen)!
2 tbsp chopped fresh tarragon
2 tbsp chopped fresh basil
1 tbsp chopped fresh chervil
1 cup grated jack cheese
1½ cup grated gruyere cheese

Method

Preheat oven to 180°C/350°F/gas mark 4
Pie crust dough — put chilled butter and shortening in mixer with the flour and salt. Use paddle attachment. Mix on medium speed until blended (3-4 minutes.) It will look like cornmeal.Then add the water & blend until the dough comes together (turn off mixer).This should only take about 10 seconds. Do not over mix! Take out of machine and chill in refrigerator for about 1 hour.

Custard — mix all ingredients.

Assembly
Roll out dough to about ¼" thick. Line bottom of 9" pie dish.
Sprinkle half of each cheese on bottom. Add crab meat. Sprinkle the herbs. Sprinkle the rest of cheese
Pour custard over all the ingredients almost to the top of dish.
Cook for 1 hour 15 minutes. Let stand for 30 minutes before serving.

"Bon appetit!"

John Travolta — Actor

SPECIAL FISH SOUP

Ingredients

A selection of fish bones, cooked heads, tails and any leftover flesh

About 1lb fish fillets
I large potato, unpeeled and diced
2 onions, chopped
2 large cloves of garlic, crushed
1 tbsp tomato puree
4oz tin peeled Italian tomatoes

fresh basil
fresh parsley
salt and black pepper
dry white wine
olive oil
butter

Method

Heat a tablespoon of olive oil in a large, heavy saucepan and add a generous knob of butter. Heat gently until the butter foams and then add half the onions and garlic. Heat gently until onions soften. Add fishy bits and continue to fry. Add in any stray bits of vegetable you've got lying around — and when it all threatens to start to stick, deglaze with a large glass of wine. Top up with plenty of cold water so that all the ingredients are well covered. Add tomato puree, salt and pepper. Simmer very gently for at least an hour. Strain and discard all the lumps — just keeping the stock to one side in a suitable jug or bowl.

Once again heat olive oil and butter in your saucepan. Add the potato, the rest of the onion and garlic. Cook for five or ten minutes until the potatoes have begun to soften. Then add in your fish fillets chopped into smallish pieces, having removed all skin. (NB if it is difficult to get skin off, don't worry. The fish will fall apart when cooked and you can hoik it out then). Stir around a bit, add fish stock, the tin of tomatoes, salt and pepper and a few fresh basil leaves torn up. Cook slowly so it is just gently simmering until the potatoes are quite soft.

Remove from heat, whiz up with a hand-held blender until the soup is thick and smooth. Check the seasoning — stir in a pinch of salt, dash of sherry and a twirl of cream as preferred. Sprinkle with chopped parsley and serve with croutons and lashings of grated cheese.

Jane Wenham-Jones — Writer & broadcaster

LENTIL SOUP

Ingredients

25g (1oz) butter
1 onion, chopped
2 garlic cloves, crushed
1 tomato, chopped
225g (8oz) red lentils
1.1ltr (2 pts) chicken stock
5ml (1 tsp) ground cumin
salt and freshly ground black pepper
lemon juice

Method

Melt butter in a large saucepan. Add the onion and garlic and cook for 5 minutes, until soft. Add the tomato and cook for 1 minute.

Wash the lentils and add to the pan with the stock. Bring to the boil and simmer for 35-45 minutes, until the lentils are soft.

Puree in a food processor or blender (or not if chunky soup is required) and return to pan. Reheat gently.

Add cumin and season to taste. Stir well and add a dash of lemon juice just before serving.

THAI PUMPKIN SOUP

Ingredients

1kg pumpkin or butternut squash, peeled, deseeded and cut into 1cm cubes
1 tbsp vegetable oil
1 onion, chopped
2½cm fresh root ginger, peeled and finely chopped
4 tsp red Thai curry paste
450ml vegetable stock
400ml coconut milk
140ml single cream
20g fresh basil, chopped

Method

Preheat oven to 180°C/350°F/gas mark 4. Place the pumpkin or butternut squash on a non-stick baking tray and season. Roast for 30 minutes, or until tender.

Meanwhile, heat the oil in a medium pan and add the onion and ginger. Cover and sauté for 10 minutes, stirring occasionally. Stir in the curry paste and cook for 1-2 minutes, then add the pumpkin, stock and coconut milk. Cover and bring to the boil, then allow to simmer for 5 minutes. Remove from heat and cool slightly.

Purée the soup in a food processor or blender in 2 batches, until smooth. Return to the pan, season to taste and reheat gently, adding a little more stock or boiling water for a thinner consistency if required.

Place the cream and chopped basil in a small basin in a pan and heat gently. Serve the soup in bowls with basil cream swirled over the top and sprinkle with freshly ground black pepper, and with crusty-granary bread on the side.

Virginia McKenna OBE — Born Free Foundation

SCRAMBLED EGGS

"This is how to make scrambled eggs! Do not laugh. When I told Ava Gardner how I made these scrambled eggs she said 'That's exactly the way Frank (Sinatra) did them.'"

Ingredients

6 eggs
butter
milk

Method

Take 6 eggs (or whatever number you want!) and crack them into a bowl.

Have standing by a frying pan with a large amount of butter in it. Add a generous amount of milk to the eggs. Get the frying pan going and whisk the eggs at the same time. When the butter is melted and very hot in the frying pan and the eggs are thoroughly whisked, pour them immediately after whisking into the frying pan and stir with a wooden spoon.

They will be done very quickly because they're in a frying pan.

You should really have, in another frying pan, some bread frying, but that is sometimes too difficult for me.

Michael Winner — Director and Author

VITALITY COCKTAIL

Ingredients

1 cup milk
2 tbsp soya protein powder
1 tbsp lecithin granules
1 raw egg
1 large banana

Method

Blend for 30 seconds
Buzz for 2 hours!

Robert Powell — Actor

SOUFFLE SUISSESSE

Ingredients

140g (5oz) butter
65g flour
700ml milk
5 egg yolks
1ltr double cream
6 egg whites
200g Gruyere or Emmental cheese

Method

Preheat the oven to 200°C/400°F/gas mark 6.

Melt 65g (2oz) butter in a small saucepan set over low heat. Using a small wire whisk, stir in the flour. Cook gently for 2 or 3 minutes, stirring continuously. Take the pan off the heat and leave the roux to cool slightly. Bring the milk to the boil, then pour it over the cooled roux, whisking all the time. Set the pan over high heat and, stirring continuously, bring the mixture to the boil and cook for 3 minutes. Take the pan off the heat and stir in the egg yolks. Season to taste with salt and pepper.

Dot the surface with 1tbsp butter, cut into small pieces to prevent a skin from forming. Set aside at room temperature

Meanwhile chill 8 round 8cm (3") tartlet tins in the refrigerator or freezer for a few minutes. Remove and immediately grease them generously with softened butter and arrange on a baking sheet.

Pour the cream into a gratin dish. Lightly salt the cream then warm it gently without allowing it to boil. Beat the egg whites with a pinch of salt until they form stiff peaks. Pour the souffle mixture into a wide mouthed bowl. Using a whisk quickly beat in one-third of the beaten egg whites then, using a spatula, carefully fold in the remainder. Using a tablespoon, heap up the mixture in the tartlet tins to form 8 large mounds.

Bake the soufflés in the preheated oven for 3 minutes until the tops begin to turn golden. Remove from the oven and, protecting your hands with a cloth, turn out each soufflé into the dish of warm cream. Sprinkle over the Gruyere or Emmental and return to the oven for 5 minutes.

Albert Roux — Chef

Notes

_____

_____

_____

_____

_____

_____

_____

_____

_____

_____

_____

_____

*"**We want** to be like you, do the things you do and take for granted."*

Vegetarian

CHAMP

"This is a delicious Irish speciality which is simple and quick to cook. It should be served with plenty of melted butter drizzling down — but the health-conscious can reduce this."

Ingredients

900g/2lb floury potatoes
spring onions
25g/1oz butter
4 tbsp milk
salt and freshly ground black pepper
knobs of butter to serve

Method

In separate pans, boil the potatoes and onions in lightly salted boiling water until tender (the onions will cook for a much shorter time than the potatoes). Drain both and mash the potatoes in a bowl with the butter and the milk. Add the onions to the potatoes and mix in with some seasoning. Heap into a bowl and make a hollow in the centre of the mash. Add extra knobs of butter and serve immediately.

PASTA PRIMAVERA

Ingredients

50g wholemeal penne
1 broccoli head
2 medium sized courgettes
2 medium sized onions

8 large mushrooms
2 large tomatoes
2 cloves of garlic
grated parmesan cheese (optional)

Method

Cook the pasta in boiling water for 12 minutes (until al dente). Drain and refresh with boiling water (removing excess starch). Break the broccoli head into florets and cook in the steamer or colander over boiling water. Steam for seven minutes approximately (so that the broccoli is cooked, but still crunchy).

Chop the onions coarsely and saute in a little butter until soft. (If you have a microwave no butter is needed. Put the onions in a bowl with about half an inch of water on the bottom. Cover with cling film and cook at a high temperature for two and a half minutes. When cooked, drain and add to the broccoli). Wash the courgettes and cut into 2" strips. Cook in the steamer for about five minutes, or boil in water until cooked but not too soft. Clean the mushrooms with a little salt and kitchen paper (or you can peel them). Place under a hot grill for a few minutes. Drain on kitchen paper. When cooked, cut into large chunks.

Concasse the tomatoes by placing them in boiling water for 10 seconds, then transferring them immediately to cold water. This allows you to remove the skin. Quarter, and cut each quarter in half again. Remove the seeds. Crush the garlic and add to the vegetables. Season with salt and pepper. Add the vegetables (except the broccoli) to the pasta and reheat gently in a saucepan. Place the broccoli back in the steamer for a minute to reheat and then carefully add to the hot pasta and vegetables. This prevents the broccoli from breaking up. Add a little grated parmesan for more flavour but this is not essential. Serve warm — not too hot. It's scrumptious and another healthy dish that children will savour.

Joan Collins — Actress and Author

THAI GREEN CURRY PASTE

The green of this curry paste comes from the fresh coriander leaves. Like all plant materials, the natural chlorophyll (green colour) oxidises in air, fading rapidly on picking and cooking. Although this paste will last for up to a week in the refrigerator, it should be used within 2 days for maximum impact, colour and flavour. It is best for the clear, hot, sour/sweet curries much beloved of the Thais.

Ingredients

15 green chillies, chopped
4 spring onions or 1 large onion, peeled and chopped
3 cloves garlic, peeled and roughly chopped
1 tbsp oil
1 tbsp chopped galangal or ginger
2 tbsp fish sauce
1 tbsp sugar
1 tsp blachan (shrimp paste) or 2 tsp dried shrimps
3 stalks of lemon grass, crushed
1 tsp ground coriander
4 tbsp or 1 bunch of fresh coriander leaves, chopped juice and grated rind of 2 limes
3 fresh kaffir lime leaves (optional)

Method

Combine all the ingredients and liquidise or process to a smooth paste in a food processor.

This can be added to any ingredients you like, for example lightly fried strips of breast of chicken, or strips of beef, green and red peppers and onions, baby sweet corn or anything else that takes your fancy.

Serve with Thai fragrant rice.

Lorraine Kelly — Presenter

NUTTY CRUMBLE-TOPPED MUSHROOMS

"I like this recipe because it is quick and easy to make in the short periods that I am at home. It is also the only mushroom dish I like as I'm not really a fan of mushrooms in general."

Ingredients

450g (1lb) parsnips, sliced
1 bunch spring onions, thickly sliced
1 green pepper de-seeded and cut into strips
190ml ($\frac{1}{3}$ pt) dry cider
150ml (¼ pt) vegetable stock
450g (1lb) white or brown mushrooms, thickly sliced
10ml (2 tsp) mild mustard
30ml (2 tbsp) cornflour
Crumble
25g (1oz) butter or margarine
40g (1½oz) wholemeal plain flour
50g (2oz) chopped mixed nuts

Method

Put parsnips, spring onions, green pepper, cider and stock into a saucepan. Cover and bring to the boil, then simmer for 5 minutes. Stir in the mushrooms and mustard. Blend cornflour with a little cold water until smooth, then stir into the pan. Bring to the boil stirring to thicken the stock. Turn into an ovenproof dish. Cool. To make the crumble, rub the fat into the flour and stir in the nuts. Sprinkle crumble over the cooled vegetables.

Cook in the oven 190°C/375°F/gas mark 5, for about 25 minutes.

Evelyn Glennie — Musican
© Mark Harrison. Good Housekeeping

CARROT CURRY

Ingredients

1½-2lb sliced fresh carrots
8fl oz fresh orange juice
water
1 tsp salt
4 tbsp butter or ghee
1 ripe banana
2-3 tbsp raisins
4-5 cardamom pods (seeds only)
1½ tsp turmeric
1½ tsp mustard seeds
4 whole cloves
1 tbsp cumin seeds
¼ tsp cayenne pepper
1½ tbsp cornflour
½ tsp prepared curry powder (optional)

Method

Scrape the carrots and slice them on a slant - not too thin. Put them in a pot with the orange juice, salt and enough water to just cover. Simmer the carrots for about five minutes.

In a large skillet, heat the butter or ghee and add it to all the spices. Heat them for a few minutes, then add the carrots in their liquid, the raisins and the banana, very thinly sliced. Simmer the curry slowly for about half an hour. If the liquid still seems too thin, take some of it out into a cup and mix it well with a little cornflour. When you have a smooth thin paste, return it to the curry and stir in. Heat a few more minutes and the curry is ready to serve.

Jasper Carrot — Comedian

ROASTED NEW POTATOES WITH THYME

Ingredients

1¾kg small new potatoes
90ml olive oil
salt and freshly ground black pepper
1 packet of fresh thyme, to serve

Method

Preheat the oven to 200°C/400°F/gas mark 6. Parboil the potatoes in salted water for 10 minutes. Drain.
Place the potatoes in a large, shallow roasting pan. Drizzle the olive oil over them, season with plenty of salt and pepper and toss them well to coat.

Roast the potatoes for 30-35 minutes, or until golden brown and cooked through. Pull off the leaves from the sprigs of thyme and toss them with the hot roasted potatoes.

Serve at once.

Ken Livingstone
Mayor of London

PAPPADELLE WITH PUMPKIN

"This is a simple pasta that is easy to assemble. The truffle oil adds to its seasonal credentials, and increases its sophistication."

Ingredients

750g (peeled weight) pumpkin or butternut squash
4 tbsp extra virgin olive oil
2 tbsp coarsely chopped sage
2 cloves garlic, thinly sliced
250g ricotta cheese
zest of 1 lemon

25g parmesan, freshly grated
truffle oil
salt and pepper
300g/400g pappadelle
sage to decorate

Method

Preheat the oven to 375°F/190°C/gas mark 5.
Peel the pumpkin, scoop out the seeds with a spoon and cut into bite-size cubes. Line a baking tray with foil, scatter over the pumpkin, season with salt and pepper and lightly drizzle with a little oil. Roast in the oven until soft and light golden brown (approx 20 minutes).
Set aside once cooked. This can be prepared in advance, but reheat before serving.
Bring a large saucepan of water to the boil for the pasta and be generous with the salt.
Pour 4 tbsp of olive oil into a sauté or frying pan and add the garlic and sage. Cook gently until the garlic has just started to turn light golden brown. Add the pumpkin and remove from heat, stirring the pumpkin to coat in the garlic and sage.
Cook the pasta according to the manufacturer's instructions. Remove a cup of pasta water just before it's cooked. Drain the pasta and add the pasta to the pumpkin. Add the ricotta, lemon zest, parmesan and the cup of pasta water and mix together. Season with a little extra salt and a generous amount of black pepper and drizzle of truffle oil.
Serve immediately with extra parmesan and truffle oil if needed.

Sophie Braimbridge
Chef

Notes

_____

_____

_____

_____

_____

_____

_____

_____

_____

_____

_____

_____

*"**We want** to have intimate relationships maybe have children."*

Main Meals

FRUITY PORK FILLETS WITH ROOT PURÉE

Ingredients

For the pork
8oz tenderloin pork fillet,
cut into ½" slices
1 tbsp cranberry or redcurrant jelly
5fl oz double cream
juice ½ lemon
salt and pepper
1 tbsp flour, seasoned with salt and pepper
2oz butter
8 ready to eat prunes soaked for at least 30 minutes in dry white wine

For the mash
8oz parsnips, cubed
8oz floury potatoes, cubed
3-4 tbsp milk
1½oz butter
salt and pepper

Method

Cook parsnips and potatoes in a large pan of boiling, salted water for 10 -12 minutes until tender. Dust the pork with the seasoned flour. Heat half the butter in a large frying pan and, when foaming, cook the pork for 1-2 minutes on each side. Remove and set aside.

Strain the wine into a hot pan and bring to the boil. Stir in the redcurrant jelly and cook for a further two minutes, until melted. Add the cream, prunes and pork, season to taste and gently simmer until the pork is cooked through.

Drain the root vegetables and mash well. Add the milk and remaining butter and whizz with an electric hand whisk until smooth and puréed, season to taste. Squeeze a little lemon juice into the pork pan and check the seasoning. Pile the mash on to serving plates and spoon over the pork mixture.

Serve with green beans.

BETTY'S HOTPOT

Ingredients

© Granada Television Ltd

1½lb (675g) neck of lamb, cubed
1½lb (675g) potatoes, peeled and thinly sliced
1 large or 2 medium onions roughly chopped
¾ pint (425ml) light stock or hot water
1 tbsp Worcestershire sauce
1 bayleaf
1 tbsp flour
1oz (25g) dripping and 1oz (25g) butter (or 2oz (50g) butter)
salt and pepper to season.

Method

Preheat the oven to 170°C/ 325°F/ gas mark 5.

Melt the dripping or butter over a high heat in a heavy-bottomed frying pan until the fat smokes. Seal the meat and continue frying until nicely browned. Remove the pieces from the pan to a deep casserole or divide among four individual high-sided, ovenproof dishes.

Turn down the heat to medium. Fry the onions in the pan juices, adding a little more butter or dripping if necessary. When the onions are soft and starting to brown, sprinkle on the flour and stir in to soak up the fat and the juices. As the flour paste starts to colour, start adding stock or water a few tablespoons at a time, stirring vigorously to avoid lumps. Gradually add the rest of the liquid. Bring to a simmer, stirring constantly, add the Worcestershire sauce and season with salt and pepper to taste.

Pour the onions and liquid over the meat and mix well. Tuck in the bayleaf (tear into four pieces if making individual hotpots).

Arrange the potatoes over the meat in over-lapping layers, seasoning each layer. Dot the top layer of potato with the remainder of the butter.

Cover the dish and place on the top shelf of the oven for 2 hours. Uncover and cook for a further 30 minutes. If the potatoes are not brown by this point, turn up the oven and cook for a further 15 minutes, or finish off under the grill, brushing the potato slices with more butter if they look too dry.

STEAK AND WINE PIE FROM JOLENE AND SID PERKS

'Freda's pies are one of the most popular choices in the Ploughman's bar at the Bull'

Ingredients

12-16oz prepared puff pastry
2½lb lean chuck steak, cubed
½lb kidney cubed
1 large onion, thinly sliced
6oz mushrooms, sliced
2 cloves garlic, crushed
3oz seasoned flour
3 tbsp sunflower oil
3½oz butter
1 pt beef stock
½ pt dry red wine
1 egg

Method

Toss the meat and kidneys in the seasoned flour. Heat the oil and 2oz butter and brown the meat. Melt the remaining butter in another pan, fry the onions for 5 minutes, and add the mushrooms and garlic and fry for another 2 minutes. Pour in the stock and wine, bring to the boil then pour over the meat and season. Cover and cook for 1½ -2 hours in a preheated oven 160°C/325°F/gas mark 3. Leave the meat to cool then place in a 3½pt pie dish with a pie funnel. Cover the pie dish with the rolled pastry and brush with beaten egg. Bake in the centre of a preheated oven 230°C/450°F/gas mark 8 for 20 minutes until golden brown.

"Enjoy with a glass of Shires!"

© The Archers BBC Radio 4

CHICKEN IN CIDER

Ingredients

4 chicken pieces
8 rashers streaky bacon
4oz mushrooms
cider
1 onion
4 eating apples
bouquet garni

Method

Fry chicken pieces in butter. Put on one side and fry diced onion and apples, bacon cut into small pieces and mushrooms. Put into casserole and lay chicken pieces on top. Cover vegetables in cider and add bouquet garni. Bake slowly in oven until chicken is tender.

Serve with new potatoes and vegetables of your choice.

Best wishes
June Whitfield

June Whitfield — Actress

CURRIED POACHED CHICKEN JAMBALAYA

Ingredients

For the poached chicken
1 tsp vegetable oil
110g/4oz drained chickpeas
1 pinch ground ginger
1 pinch medium curry powder
1 pinch ground turmeric
1 pinch cayenne
1 pinch cumin seeds, crushed
1 chicken breast, skinned

For the Jambalaya
85g/3oz American easy cook rice
1 tbsp vegetable oil
85g/3oz okra, topped and halved lengthways
½ red pepper, de-seeded and sliced
$1/3$ small coconut, shelled and chopped
2 tsp chopped fresh tarragon, salt and freshly ground black pepper

Method

Heat the oil for the chickpeas in a small frying pan. Fry the chickpeas with the spices for 2-3 minutes. Transfer to a food processor and puree. Half fill a medium pan with water and bring to the boil. Reduce the heat to a simmer, place the chicken between two sheets of cling film and, using a meat mallet, bash into an escalope.
Place the curried chickpea puree along the length of the chicken. Fold the ends of the chicken in, then roll to enclose the chickpea mixture. Wrap the chicken tightly in cling film to form a sausage shape, tie the ends, then poach for 12-14 minutes or until the chicken is firm and cooked through. Cook the rice as per the packet instructions.
Heat the oil for the stir-fry in a wok. Stir-fry the vegetables and coconut for 4-5 minutes or until just beginning to soften.
Carefully remove the chicken from the water and take off the cling film. Slice the stuffed chicken on the diagonal.
Drain the rice and stir it into the vegetable mixture with the tarragon. Season and serve the sliced chicken on a bed of the vegetable rice.

GREAT BRITAIN

ATHLETICS TEAM

Jamie Baulch — Athlete

EASY STIR-FRY CHICKEN

"I really enjoy stir-fries as they are quick and easy and fit well with my athletics diet."

Ingredients

4oz mangetout
4oz baby sweetcorn
4 skinless, boneless chicken breasts, cut into peices
2½cm root ginger
spring onions
2 carrots, peeled and cut into matchsticks
2 tbsp olive oil

Sauce
150ml chicken stock
1 tbsp soft, dark brown sugar
1 tbsp cornflour
1 tbsp soy sauce

Method

Heat wok, when the wok is steaming add the oil. Add the chicken and stir fry for 7-8 minutes, or until golden. Transfer chicken to a plate and keep warm.
Stir fry the ginger, spring onions and carrots for 2 minutes, add the sweetcorn, and mangetout and cook for a further 1 minute.
Whisk together the sauce ingredients until smooth and well blended.
Return the chicken pieces to the pan, add the sauce and bring to the boil, simmer for a couple of minutes then remove and serve over cooked noodles or rice.

Tanni Grey-Thompson — Athlete

TUTU CHICKEN

Ingredients

3 potatoes
1 chicken cut in pieces
75g (3oz) seasoned flour
30ml (2 tbsp) vegetable oil
2 onions chopped
1 green pepper sliced
2 large tomatoes, skinned and chopped
400g (14oz) can tomato puree
15ml (1 tbsp) curry paste
5ml (1 tsp) Tabasco sauce
1 chicken stock cube
600ml (1 pt) water

Method

Boil the potatoes for ten minutes until half cooked. Peel and slice.
Coat chicken in seasoned flour. Heat oil in frying pan and brown. Remove from pan.
Add onions and green pepper and cook until soft.
Add 4-5 tbsp of the remaining flour to the pan and cook for 1 minute.
Add tomato puree, curry paste, Tabasco sauce, stock and sufficient water to make a thick sauce.
Put the chicken pieces in a large casserole, cover with the sliced potatoes and the vegetables.
Cover the casserole and bake at 150°C/300°F/gas mark 2 for an hour.
Serve with rice and a salad.

Rev. Desmond Tutu — Archbishop

ENCHILLADAS

Ingredients

500g mince
2 large peppers (red & green)
1 courgette
6 tortilla wraps
1 tin chopped tomatoes
1 tin kidney beans in chilli sauce
1-2 tsp mild curry powder
2 handfuls grated cheese (low fat)

Method

Brown the mince then drain away the fat
Chop up the courgette & peppers into fine pieces and stir fry with the mince
Add the chopped tomato and kidney beans with chilli sauce and curry powder. Stir well and simmer for 10 minutes.
Divide the mince mixture between 6 tortillas and make into a filled wrap, wrapping the corners over to make filled pockets.
Lay each wrap side by side on to an ovenproof dish.
Spoon any leftover filling on to the wraps plus the grated cheese.
Bake in the oven for 15 minutes (220˚C/400˚F/gas mark 8) or until lightly browned.

"Enjoy!"

Goldie Sayers — Athlete

FRITATA

Ingredients

Can use anything you want to use up!

Method

Fry a medium onion in a little oil until soft. Then add whatever you like: potatoes, tomatoes, peppers, ham, salami, chopped vegetables.
The frying pan should be large – when you have got a few things warmed in the pan remove from the heat.
Grate 4oz of cheddar cheese.
Take 6 eggs and beat in a bowl with some salt and pepper.
Pour into the pan. Sprinkle cheese on top and put under the grill for 10 minutes until nicely risen and crispy.
Serve with warm fresh bread and salad.

Linda Bellingham — Actress

FISH PIE

Ingredients

2lb haddock or cod (smoked fish will give a much stronger flavour)
1 pt milk
4oz butter
2oz flour
4 hard boiled eggs, chopped
4 tbsp fresh chopped parsley
2 tbs fresh lemon juice
salt and black pepper
2lb potatoes boiled and mashed with butter, milk, salt and pepper

Method

Place fish in shallow baking dish, pour over half the milk and bake for 15 mins at 200°C/400°F/gas mark 6. Flake into large pieces.
Make a white sauce, melt butter in pan, add flour, stir in remaining milk including fish liquid and salt and pepper.
Mix to a smooth consistency and cook for 2 mins.
Add flaked fish to sauce, together with eggs, parsley, lemon and salt and pepper.
Put fish mixture into baking dish large enough to hold 2 pints.
Spread the creamed potatoes over the top and fork a pattern on fish pie.
Bake in oven at 200°C/400°F/gas mark 6 for about 30 minutes until golden brown. Do not let the mixture boil. Top with sprig parsley. Serve with fresh vegetables.

Esther Rantzen — Presenter

FORSYTH'S STEAK DIJON

As formerly served at the Wig and Pen Club in London

Ingredients

sirloin steak
English mustard
Demerara sugar

Method

Grill both sides of a sirloin steak.
On one side spread a generous amount of English mustard.
Sprinkle demerara sugar on top of the mustard, again be very generous.
Put under a very hot grill until the sugar starts to bubble and caramelise.
Serve with new potatoes and a salad or vegetables of your choice.

"Hope you enjoy it!"

Bruce Forsyth — Comedian and Presenter

SPAGHETTI BOLOGNESE

Here's a delicious low-fat version of a favourite family dish. Dry-frying the minced beef and draining off the fat saves a lot of calories.

Ingredients

450g (1lb) lean minced beef
2 garlic cloves, crushed
1 large onion, finely chopped
2 medium carrots, finely grated
2 beef stock cubes
800g (28oz) chopped tomatoes

4 tbsp tomato puree
1 tbsp chopped fresh oregano
1 vegetable stock cube
350g (12oz) spaghetti (dry weight)
salt and freshly ground black pepper
chopped fresh herbs to garnish

Method

Dry-fry the minced beef in a non-stick pan until it starts to change colour.
Remove the mince from the pan and drain through a colander. Wipe out the pan with kitchen paper.
Return the drained mince to the pan, add the garlic and onion and cook for 2-3 minutes, stirring well. Add the carrots and crumble the beef stock cubes over the top. Add the tomatoes, tomato puree and oregano and mix well to allow the stock cubes to dissolve.
Reduce the heat to a gentle simmer and season well with black pepper. Cover the pan with a lid and simmer gently for 30 minutes until the sauce thickens.
Meanwhile, bring a large pan of water to the boil and add a vegetable stock cube.
Add the spaghetti and cook until it is tender but still slightly firm in the centre.
Drain thoroughly.
Arrange the spaghetti on 4 warmed plates, pour the sauce on the top and serve garnished with fresh herbs.

Rosemary Conely — Diet and Health Expert

SPICY CHICKEN TORTILLAS

Ingredients

1 red onion, sliced
1 red pepper, halved, seeded and sliced
1 tbsp oil
250g/9oz cooked chicken, cut into strips
1½ tsp Jamaican jerk seasoning
4 ready-made flour tortillas
4 tbsp soured cream or tomato salsa or relish
4 tbsp grated cheese
4 tbsp ready-made guacamole
Cayenne pepper, for sprinkling
green salad, to serve

Method

Fry the onion and red pepper in the oil for 5 minutes. Add the chicken and jerk seasoning and stir-fry for 5 minutes until the chicken is hot. Preheat the grill to hot.

Warm the tortillas, then spread each one with soured cream, tomato salsa or relish. Add the chicken mixture and roll up. Top with the grated cheese and grill briefly until just melted. Serve topped with guacamole, sprinkled with cayenne pepper, and a green salad.

Jane Asher — Chef and Author

THAI RISOTTO WITH AUBERGINE

"Creamy rice flavoured with lemon grass, ginger, chilli and coconut milk — simply heavenly!"

Ingredients

75g butter
1 onion, peeled and chopped
2 sticks lemon grass
½ tsp curry powder
200g pumpkin, cut into cubes
100ml dry white wine
900ml hot vegetable stock
200ml unsweetened coconut milk
3 sliced spring onions and fresh coconut shavings, to garnish

1 clove garlic, crushed
1 red chilli, deseeded and chopped
1 tsp freshly chopped root ginger
1 aubergine, cut into chunks
250g arborio (risotto) rice
1 tbsp freshly chopped mint
100g shitake mushrooms, sliced
banana or vine leaves (optional)

Method

Melt half the butter in a heavy-based pan, add the onion, garlic, lemon grass, chilli, curry powder and ginger, and cook gently for 3-4 minutes, stirring occasionally, until tender. Add pumpkin, aubergine and rice and cook for a further minute. Add the wine and a little of the stock and cook, stirring occasionally, until the liquid has been absorbed into the rice.

Repeat this process with the remaining stock for about 25 minutes until the rice is tender but firm to the bite — towards the end of the cooking time, add the stock in smaller quantities. Keep checking to see if the rice is cooked. You may have some stock left over. Add coconut milk and mint, then stir. The consistency of the risotto should be fairly loose. Season, set aside and cover to keep warm.

Melt remaining butter in a pan, add mushrooms and cook for 4 minutes until golden. Arrange risotto on banana leaves, top with mushrooms, garnish and serve with fruit chutney or chilli soy dip.

Penny Smith — Presenter

Notes

_____

_____

_____

_____

_____

_____

_____

_____

_____

_____

_____

_____

_____

*"**We want** to choose who we live with and where — just like you can."*

Desserts

BANOFFEE PIE

Ingredients

large packet digestive biscuits
½lb melted unsalted butter
½ tsp dried ginger
1 tin condensed milk boiled for 2½ hours (then cooled) in the can.
10-12 bananas
1½ pt double cream
2oz castor sugar
1oz dark chocolate

Method

Boil the unopened tin of condensed milk in a pan of water for 2½ hours and leave to cool down for at least 6 hours before opening.
Note: Do not allow to boil dry as the tin will explode.
Biscuit Base:
Place biscuits into a robo chef and grind until crumbed, add dried ginger and then slowly add melted butter.
Place the mixture into a loose bottomed flan dish and allow to set in the fridge for approx. half hour.
Open the tin of condensed milk carefully. This will be set. Now spread onto the base.
Slice bananas onto this (use your judgement) as many or as little as you like.
Whip up the double cream with the caster sugar and pipe all over the bananas.
Grate the dark chocolate over the cream and put in the fridge
until ready to serve.

"Enjoy!"

Carole Smillie — Presenter

BANOFFEE PIE

Ingredients

About ½ packet digestive and/or ginger biscuits.
2oz butter
1 tbsp sugar (optional)
1 tin condensed milk
3 bananas, sliced lengthwise
1 pt whipping cream, whipped

Method

The day before, place unopened can of condensed milk into a pan of water and boil for three hours - don't let it boil dry whatever you do. Allow to cool. Make biscuit base by turning the biscuits into crumbs, melting the butter in the microwave (only about 30 seconds), mixing the two together with the sugar, if using, and pressing down into a flan dish. Leave in the fridge to harden.

Next day, open the can of milk, which will have turned to toffee, and spread it over the biscuit base — which will try and stick to the toffee, so just swoosh it round as best you can. Top this with the sliced bananas, and instantly with the cream (if you hang about, the bananas will go brown and ucky). Refrigerate until wanted.

I have also made this very successfully with peaches for someone who is allergic to bananas; if you use fresh peaches, pour boiling water over them for a minute to enable them to be peeled easily. Drained tinned peaches are fine, too.

BLACKBERRY AND APPLE TRIFLE

Ingredients

½ pt whipping cream
1lb (450g) desert apples
8oz (225g) blackberries
4 tbsp water
4-6 oz (110-175g) castor sugar
4 trifle sponges
1 pt Bird's custard made up thickly

Method

Peel, core and slice the apples and pick over the blackberries. Put the sliced apples into a pan with the water and cook over a low heat until they're half cooked. Add the sugar and blackberries and cook till tender and juice has formed. Remove from heat.

Break trifle sponges and place in the bottom of a glass serving dish. Spoon fruit over making sure the sponge is well soaked in juice.

Set dish aside and make up custard using a little extra custard powder to make it thick.

When cool spread over the fruit.

Whip cream until it peaks (you can add a little castor sugar and a few drops of vanilla essence to the cream if you wish).

Spread over the custard.

Decorate with a few firm blackberries and toasted almond flakes.

Chill before serving.

This recipes can be used with other fruit such as pears, raspberries etc.

Good wishes
Wendy
Craig

Wendy Craig — Actress

MY MUM'S BLACKBERRY PURÉE

This is something very simple, yet to me, even now that I am (nearly) grown-up, this is still the most delicious substance known to man.

My Mum made it like this:

First pick the blackberries while they are at their best, in late Summer. Only use the ones which are ready to be picked - these are black all over, and come off the plant with only a gentle pull. Wear covering on the hands and arms - the bramble bushes are vicious! About two hundred luscious fat berries is a good number to make enough Puree for two luxury helpings, or to store in the fridge, to sip at for treats over a week or so.

Put the blackberries in a pan with a teaspoon of water to get them started, and a couple or three tablespoons of sugar (this is where it gets naughty), though you can adjust this amount of sweetening to taste. Gently bring to boiling point, stirring with a wooden spoon which you don't mind getting stained dark purple. Turn the flame to low, and keep stirring and squashing the berries until the liquid becomes an even paste — not longer than 5 minutes or so anyway, because Vitamin C doesn't survive very long at 100°C.

Now if you'd had a couple of freshly scrumped Bramley's cooking apples, they could have been chopped up and put in the pan with the berries, for a thicker texture, greater volume of resulting purée, and an extra tang. But blackberries on their own give the purest flavour.

Remove the pan from the heat and pour into a metal sieve, over a glass or china bowl. Use the wooden spoon to churn the paste around, squashing the juice through and leaving the seeds behind.

The pure red Elixir can now be eaten or put in the fridge. It tastes really fabulous poured over ice cream, or the "Junket" my Mum used to make (a kind of vanilla blancmange), or as a sauce for fresh fruits, or just spooned slowly into the mouth as a wicked pleasure. My daughter also enjoys the puree frozen into an iced lolly.

Warning - this stuff stains everything it touches - wear a napkin - and is very acidic - go gently if your stomach is sensitive. But the flavour...it's a killer... guaranteed to blast your taste-buds into space..!

Brian May — Musican

CHERRY CHEESECAKE

Ingredients

4oz digestive biscuits
3oz margarine
8oz Philadelphia cream cheese
¾ cup icing sugar
dash vanilla essence
¼ pt double cream
1 tin cherry pie filling

Method

Crush biscuits and add to melted margarine to make base.
Beat all other ingredients together.
Pour on to biscuit base.
Add tin of cherry pie filling on top.

"This is quick, simple to make - and perfectly delicious!"

Alan Titchmarsh — Gardener and Presenter

CRÈME BRÛLÉE

"My method is none too professional but it works…"

Ingredients

4-6 yolks according to size of eggs
½ pt single cream
½ pt double cream (or pint double cream)
1 tsp vanilla essence
1 dsp castor sugar
¼lb approx castor sugar for the topping

Method

Heat the creams with the vanilla essence in a large, heavy bottomed saucepan. Lightly beat the egg yolks with the dessertspoon of castor sugar and pour on the scalding cream. Return to pan and stir continuously (this needs a touch of dedication) over a very low heat till the mixture coats the sides of the pan and has a thicker consistency. It will become thicker still when cold.

Pour into a shallow heatproof dish and allow to cool. Chill for several hours, or preferably overnight. Cover the chilled cream — it might have formed a very slight skin, with a generous and even layer of castor sugar. There should be no cream showing through underneath. Place the dish near the top of a grill pre-heated to maximum and watch it like a hawk. When it begins to turn rich brown in patches, whip it out and chill all over again. The top will be like sheet ice but will crack when attacked with a spoon.

Michael Howard — Leader of the opposition

PAVLOVA

Ingredients

3 egg whites
150g (6oz) caster sugar
½ tsp vanilla essence
½ tsp vinegar
1 tsp cornflour
250ml (½pt) whipped cream
fresh strawberries, raspberries, pineapple or fruit of your choice

Method

Draw an 18cm (7") circle on non-stick paper and place it on a baking sheet. Beat the egg whites until very stiff. Beat in the sugar gradually. Add the vanilla essence, vinegar and cornflour. Spread the meringue mixture over the circle, making a hollow in the centre. Leave cooked meringue in oven to cool completely before peeling off paper. Pile whipped cream in the centre and top with fruit.

Oven temperature: 140°C/275°F/gas mark 1.

Johnny Ball
Presenter

CRANNACHAN

To make this delicious Scottish pudding you will need:

Ingredients

A punnet of raspberries (roughly 170g)
8 tbsp pinhead oatmeal
500ml creme fraiche
4 tbsp honey
4 tbsp orange juice

Method

Pinhead oatmeal is fine porridge oats but if you can't find it in your local supermarket, try a health food shop.

Toast the oatmeal by spreading it onto a baking sheet and put it In a medium oven for roughly 10 minutes.

Put the creme fraiche into a bowl and stir in the toasted oatmeal. Add the clear honey followed by the of orange juice. Stir gently.

Put 4 raspberries aside for decoration and put the remaining fruit into a blender and zap until it turns into a smooth puree.

Fill 4 glasses starting with a layer of raspberries followed by the cream concoction and keep going until everything has been used up. Decorate the top of each pudding with one of the raspberries that were set aside.

Serve immediately.

© BBC Television

EGGY BREAD

Ingredients

thick sliced bread
1 egg, beaten
milk
brown sugar
1 banana
cinnamon

Method

Soak nice thick slice in egg beaten with a little milk, sprinkle with cinnamon.

Fry eggy bread in butter, while this takes just a few minutes, mash a banana.

When bread is nicely brown on both sides spread banana on the top, sprinkle with brown sugar and pop under the grill and keep your eye on it. The sugar melts on the banana.

"Y voila!"

Lionel Blair — Presenter

ETON MESS

Ingredients

500g strawberries
300ml double cream
2 meringues
2 tbsp Grand Marnier

Method

Reserving a few strawberries for decoration, cut the remainder into halves and pour on the Grand Marnier. Leave for about 2 hours. Whip the double cream until firm but not too thick. Crumble the meringues and mix with the strawberries and cream.

Serve in individual glass dishes and decorate with the reserved strawberries.

"The meringue can go soft if left so eat immediately. You'll want to anyway!"

Best wishes;
Richard Wilson

Richard Wilson — Actor
© Andy Gotts

EVERYDAY SUNDAE

Ingredients

fruit yoghurt
berries (raspberries, strawberries or blueberries)
chopped nuts
crunchy breakfast cereal

Method

Take one of those fruity yoghurt things.
In a glass put in a layer of any berries you fancy.
Then a layer of yoghurt.
Then a layer of chopped nuts,
Then more yoghurt.
Then a layer of crunchy breakfast cereal.
That's it.
And it's healthy too.

FROZEN LEMON TORTE

Ingredients

4 large eggs separated
8oz caster sugar
10fl oz double cream
1½ tbsp grated lemon zest (or orange)
4fl oz lemon juice (or 3oz frozen orange juice* + 1oz lemon)
1 packet langue du chat biscuits
1 loaf tin lined with foil or spring clip cake tin of similar volume

Method

Beat egg whites until stiff and gradually add 6oz of the sugar until forms glossy peaks.
Blend yolks with remainder of the sugar, grated rind and juice until the sugar has dissolved.
Whip cream until stiffish (same texture as egg whites).
Fold yolk mixture into cream and then fold that into the egg whites making sure everything is well mixed without beating out the air (the liquid sometimes sinks to the bottom!)
Stand the biscuits round the edge of your tin (pour a little of the mixture in first which stops them falling over!) and then pour rest of mixture into the middle. Freeze till needed and turn out. (The top often looks better than the bottom so invert it onto a plate and invert it again on to the dish you have chosen.

Decorate - with pile of finely grated lemon or orange rind which has been boiled briefly in water to remove bitterness.
Serve - IMMEDIATELY on its own or with raspberries or strawberries.
* Ordinary orange juice is not strong enough so use the small drum of concentrated frozen orange juice from the supermarket.

NB. The mixture is the texture of soft scoop icecream so you can prepare extra and place it in a plastic box - great for those unexpected guests!

The Right Hon. Anne Widdecombe — MP
© Douglas Morrison

FRENCH LEMON TART

Ingredients

1 portion puff pastry uncooked
grated rind & juice of 1-2 lemons (depending on how lemony you like things)
1 whole egg
4oz sugar
2oz melted butter

Method

Roll out pastry fairly thinly to line a 9" round or 11" by 7" oblong flan dish.
In a bowl beat the whole egg with the sugar till light and frothy; beat in the rind & juice of lemon; add the melted butter and mix well.
Pour into flan dish and cook in preheated oven at 200°C /400°F/gas mark 6 until pastry is cooked and filling is dark golden — about 25-30 minutes.

Serve with creme fraiche or double cream.

PUDDING - NO - NAUGHTY

Fruit.
Cut up.
Put on plate.

HANKS PUDDING

Ingredients

1 large carton natural yoghurt
1 large carton double cream
3 tins of raspberries
dark muscovado sugar

Method

Drain raspberries and pour into serving bowl.
Mix yoghurt and cream until thick and pour onto the raspberries.
Sprinkle the sugar on top to cover.

Best Wishes
Richard Dunwood

Richard Dunwoody — Jockey

"I love chocolate and I avoid not eating it whenever I can. I really don't mind its hue of brown and I even go for white. Even if pressed for a particular manufacturer I couldn't possibly express a preference although I do like to support fairly traded chocolate products. So my favourite puddings will always have a chocolaty theme."

"Hence one of my dilemmas — copyright and favouring a brand —forgive the pun."

"So what I will divulge is one of my private little indulgences:

I get a huge bowl, fill it not quite full of ice cream, (a good strongly flavoured vanilla) and on it I empty out several pots of chocolate fromage frais. I sit down in front of the telly and very slowly empty the bowl of its entire contents, using a spoon of course. I gently sweep my finger around the edges and refill immediately."

Jo Brand — Comedienne

PANCAKES

Ingredients

pancakes
fruit
ice cream
sugar or syrup

Method

Right, make yourself a pancake, leave it open. Place any fruit you like inside and get yourself a very large tub of ice cream. I like Rum & Raisin but you can use whatever. Close the pancake with a light dusting of sugar or syrup.

"Oh, I want one now!"

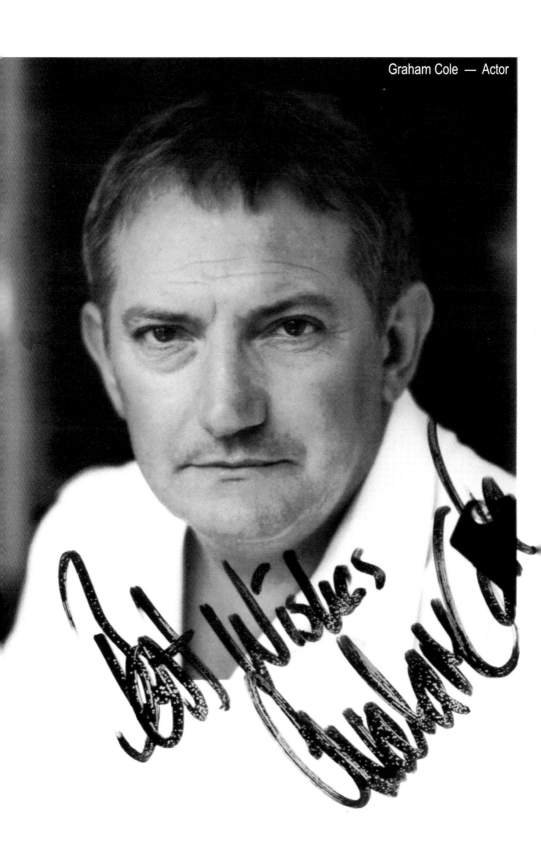

Graham Cole — Actor

PANNA COTTA WITH SPICED ORANGES

Ingredients

2pt double cream
2 vanilla pods
2 oranges, (zest)
4 leaves of gelatine
5oz caster sugar
120ml milk
80ml vodka or grappa
8 oranges

1 cinnamon stick
3 large pinches of allspice
100ml water
100g caster sugar
150g caster sugar (for the sugar cage)
100g fresh redcurrants
1 small bunch of fresh mint

Method

Firstly, soak the gelatine in the milk and leave to one side. Then place the orange zest, split vanilla pods and 5oz caster sugar in a pan. Add 800ml of the cream and bring to the boil. Simmer until the mixture is reduced by a third.

While the cream is reducing, remove the gelatine from the milk and place the milk in a pan to warm gently. Once it is warm add the soaked gelatine and stir to dissolve. Add to the warm cream and pass through a sieve and leave to cool.

Lightly whip the remaining cream and fold into the setting mixture, together with the vodka. Pour the mixture into about 6 ramekins or similar sized moulds and place in the fridge to set.

While setting, peel the oranges with a peeler and place the peel in a pan. Remove the pith with a knife and segment the oranges and add to the pan with the peel. Add the spices, water and sugar and bring to the boil. Gently simmer for about 15 minutes and leave to cool.

Remove the Panna Cotta from the fridge and using a knife slide it around the edge to loosen. Tip them out into the middle of the plates and spoon the oranges around the edge. Garnish with some redcurrants and a sugar cage over the top and serve.

James Martin — Chef

PASSION FRUIT WATER ICE

Ingredients

1pt water
8oz caster sugar
1 egg white
8 passion fruits

Method

Dissolve the sugar in the water over a low gas. Boil gently for 10 minutes.
Leave to cool.
Cut passion fruits in half and scoop out the flesh, put into a fine sieve and
pass through, leaving all the black pips behind.
Add juice to cooled sugar syrup and pour into container
Place in freezer and leave until just beginning to freeze around the edges.
Add whisked egg white and return to freezer.

Serve this delicious water ice in pretty wine glasses with a wafer biscuit
on top.

"Before I retired from athletics I found this very refreshing after a hard
training session."

Sally Gunnell — Athlete and Presenter

MAGIC JELLY

Make up a packet jelly and follow the instructions on the packet.
Where the instructions say to use cold water, substitute the water with fizzy lemonade.

"When you eat it, if you press the jelly onto the roof of your mouth it fizzes...magic!"

Paul Daniels — Magician

PEACHES WITH AMARETTO BISCUITS

Ingredients

fresh peaches
plum jam
Amaretto biscuits
white or rosé wine
double cream

Method

Halve peaches horizontally and remove stone. Put jam in the hole. Crush amaretti biscuits and place on top.
Put into a baking dish with some white or rosé wine — an inch or so — and bake in oven 190°C/375°F/gas mark 5 for around 30 minutes.
Serve warm with chilled double cream.

"Very simple and delicious."

Julia McKenzie — Actress

PECAN CREAM PIE

This is my favourite recipe. I first had Pecan Pie in Key West in Florida and I asked the chef for his recipe.

Ingredients

1½ cups plain flour
¼ cup castor sugar
125g butter
1 egg yolk
1 tbsp cold water (approx)
2 tsp castor sugar, extra
Filling
250g pecans
300ml thickened cream
2 tbsp honey

Method

Sift flour, add sugar, rub in butter, add egg yolk and enough water to mix to a firm dough.
Refrigerate for 30 minutes.
Roll half pastry to fit base and side of 23cm flan tin.
Combine all filling ingredients and add filling.
Cover with remaining pastry; trim edges, brush with water and sprinkle with extra castor sugar.
Cook in moderately hot oven for 10 minutes.
Reduce heat to moderate and bake for further 20 minutes until golden brown.
Serve warm with cream.

"MMmmmm! Delicious!"

Neil Buchannan — Presenter

RICH CHOCOLATE ICE CREAM

"My family love anything with chocolate in it. Here is a delicious recipe for one of our favourite ways of enjoying a chocolate dessert."

Ingredients

6 egg yolks
125g (4oz) caster sugar
900ml (1½pt) double cream
5ml (1 tsp) vanilla essence
325g (12oz) plain chocolate

Method

Whisk the egg yolks and caster sugar together until the mixture is very light and pale.

Break the plain chocolate into the mixture and heat gently, stirring all the time, until the mixture coats the back of a wooden spoon and the chocolate is completely melted. It is important that you DO NOT ALLOW THE MIXTURE TO BOIL. Once this is done, then let it cool.

Pour the cooled chocolate mixture into a freezer-proof container and freeze for about 5 hours. I always find that adding 2 tablespoons of Grand Marnier to the mixture before freezing helps to keep it more moist.

Put in the fridge about 20 minutes before serving with some nice fruit, like strawberries done in a raspberry coulis.

ROCKY ROAD ICE CREAM

"This is not for the cowardly, it has a zillion calories but who cares, worry about it later. You will need to be in possession of an ice cream machine. Mine is a small twenty pound affair that serves its purpose brilliantly. The marshmallows and the almonds need to be added to taste so I haven't stated a specific amount."

Ingredients

200g good quality plain chocolate (good old Bournville would do it)
1 large pot double cream
1 bag marshmallows
small bag whole almonds
½ tsp vanilla essence.
1 dsp acacia honey

Method

Carefully melt the chocolate in a bowl placed on a pan of gently simmering water, not boiling as this can spoil the chocolate.
When melted add the double cream (it mustn't be whipped). Stir the two ingredients together. Halve the almonds widthways or lengthways, widthways gives them more bite (you can toast them beforehand if this is what you would prefer). You will only need about half the bag unless like me you love almonds and you want to add the lot!
Cut the marshmallows into quarters. I love marshmallows and would happily add the whole bag, but you may only need half the bag.
Pour the chocolate and cream mixture into an ice cream machine and add the almonds. After about five minutes, when the mixture has cooled considerably, add the marshmallows. It will take about 20 minutes for the mixture to freeze, and then if I were you I'd eat the lot as it's far too good to put in the freezer until another day.

"The next day go jogging for twenty minutes and make again!"

SUMMER PUDDING

Ingredients

300g blackcurrants
300g redcurrants
400g raspberries
125g castor sugar
Day old sliced white bread
(avoid strawberries as they have the wrong texture)

Method

Divide the sugar into two equal measures and simmer the redcurrants and blackcurrants separately in a saucepan with the sugar and just enough water to prevent burning. Add the raspberries.

Line the bottom and sides of a 1½ltr pudding bowl with sliced white bread and fill with the fruit mixture, remembering to set aside a little juice for later. I like to add a touch of Creme de Peche liqueur here to give it that extra kick!

Seal with a further circle of sliced white bread and cover with a heavy plate.
Refrigerate for 24 hours, turn out and pour the remaining juice over.
Serve immediately with organic cream.

© adapted from a recipe by Monty Don

TRANSKEI MUD

Ingredients

405g can condensed milk
280ml double cream
200g digestive biscuits
100g mint chocolate (such as Aero), grated
Boil the can of condensed milk unopened, and completely covered with water at all times, for about two hours. Allow it to cool fully, or overnight.

Method

Whisk the double cream until it stands in soft peaks. Slowly add the caramelised milk, one spoonful at a time. Mix thoroughly.
Grate all the chocolate, then reserving a little for decoration, add it to the mixture and stir in.
Layer the mixture into a glass serving dish, alternating with the digestive biscuits, making three layers of each. Refrigerate overnight. Sprinkle over the remaining chocolate before serving.
(If feeling particularly indulgent, whip a second carton of double cream until stiff, and spread this over the pudding before decorating with remaining chocolate.)

Serve in small portions, as the pudding is very rich.

Cliff Richard — Singer

YOGHURT AND GINGER

Ingredients

Greek yoghurt
stem ginger

"I just adore greek yoghurt with some chopped stem ginger on top and some juice trickled over."

Honor Blackman — Actress

GINGER COOKIES WITH HONEYCOMB ICE CREAM

Ingredients

175g butter
¾ cup castor sugar
1½ cups plain flour
2-3 heaped tsp ginger powder
1 cup chopped ginger

Method

Blend ingredients together with fork or pastry blender. Roll mixture into ¾cm thickness and cut with cookie cutter.
Cook extremely slowly on a baking tray at 100-125°C/210-250°F/gas mark 1 for 1 hour.
When cookies have cooled, place one on the bottom, a scoop of ice cream in the middle and a second cookie on top — garnish with a flower from the garden.

"It's a favourite because it's simple and delicious!"

Dame Kiri Te Kanawa - Soprano
© John Swannell

Notes

"**We want** to go out to work, just like you."

Puddings

APPLE AND RHUBARB ALMOND SPONGE

Ingredients

1lb cooking apples
1lb rhubarb
grated rind and juice of 1 orange
3oz demerara sugar
2oz sultanas

Sponge
3oz butter
3oz sugar
2 eggs
a few drops of almond essence
3oz self-raising flour
1oz ground almonds
salt
a little milk

Method

Peel and slice apples.
Wash and cut rhubarb into 1" pieces.
Put in a saucepan with orange juice and rind, sugar and sultanas.
Simmer for about 15 minutes.
Pour into greased ovenproof dish.

Sponge Topping
Cream butter and sugar.
Add eggs and almond essence.
Mix in flour, ground almonds and salt.
Add a little milk to make a dropping consistency. Then spoon over the fruit and sprinkle the top with flaked almonds.

Cook at 180°C/350°F/gas mark 4 for 35-40 minutes.
Serve hot with custard or cream.

Sir Richard Branson — Entrepreneur

APPLE FLAPJACK PUDDING

Ingredients

1½lb eating apples
2oz demerara sugar
grated rind and juice of 1 lemon
5oz dark muscovado sugar
5oz butter

4 tbsp golden syrup
4oz self-raising wholemeal flour
8oz porridge oats
2 tsp ground cinnamon
2 eggs, beaten

Method

Quarter, peel and core the apples; cut each quarter into three slices. Place in a pan with the Demerara sugar, lemon rind and juice. Heat gently, then cook for 5 minutes until the apples are just starting to soften. Remove from the pan with a slotted spoon, then boil the sauce until reduced and thickened. Pour the sauce over the apples.

Measure the muscovado sugar, butter and syrup into a small pan. Heat gently until the butter has melted, then cool slightly. In a mixing bowl, mix together the flour, oats and cinnamon. Make a well in the centre and pour in the melted mixture and eggs, stirring thoroughly to make a smooth batter.

Spread two-thirds of the mixture evenly over the base and sides of a buttered 2½ pint pudding basin. Fill with the apples and spread the remaining mixture over the top. Cover with greaseproof paper and foil; steam for 2 hours.

Cool in the basin for 10 minutes, then turn out and serve with custard.

Sandi Toksvig — Presenter
© Catherine Shakespear Lane

BAKED ALASKA

Ingredients

1 large sponge cake
1 block ice cream
about 4-6oz fresh canned or frozen fruit

For the meringue
4-5 egg whites
Sugar — 1-2oz per egg white

Method

Choose an ovenproof dish so the sweet can be served and baked in the same container. Place the sponge cake on this, soaking with a little fruit syrup if using canned or frozen fruit. Top with the very firm block of ice cream and fruit.

Make the meringue mixture by whisking the egg whites until very stiff, then folding the sugar in gradually. Pile or pipe the meringue mixture over the whole of the sponge cake and ice cream mixture — taking care no ice cream is left uncovered, otherwise it will melt.

Put into a very hot oven (220°C/475°F/gas mark 8-9) for about 3 minutes only, until golden brown. Remove from the oven and serve at once or leave no longer than 30 minutes before serving.

"Delicious!"

Best Wishes,

David Suchet OBE — Actor

BANANA SURPRISE

"This is really easy".

Ingredients

bananas
honey or golden syrup
tinfoil for wrapping

Method

Take a banana, split the skin with a knife all the way down one side.
Place on a square of tin foil (big enough to wrap banana).
Open up the split and pour in honey or golden syrup.
Place in a hot oven (about 180˚C/350°F/gas mark 4) and bake for about 15 minutes.

"It's even better on a BBQ!"

Davina McCall — Presenter

BREAD AND BUTTER PUDDING

Ingredients

½ pint (275ml) milk
70ml double cream
grated rind of half a small lemon
2oz (50g) castor sugar
3 eggs
Pannetone cake
½oz (10g) candied lemon or orange peel, finely chopped
2oz (50)g currants
freshly-grated nutmeg

Method

Heat oven to 180°C/350°F/gas mark 4

Butter a 2 pint oblong enamel baking dish.
Slice the Pannetone and butter it. Put one layer on the base of the dish, sprinkle with the candied peel and half the currants. Put another layer of Pannetone in the dish and sprinkle with the rest of the currants.

Put the milk and cream together in a measuring jug, stir in the lemon peel and sugar. Whisk the eggs in a small basin and add to the milk mixture. Pour the whole lot over the Pannetone and sprinkle with freshly grated nutmeg.

Bake in the oven for 30-40 minutes. Serve warm.

"This is delicious and provides the perfect solution for what to do with those dry Italian cakes you get given at Christmas!"

Dame Judi Dench — Actress

BREAD AND BUTTER PUDDING

Ingredients

12 medium slices white bread
300 ml (½ pint) milk
50g (2oz) unsalted butter, softened
300 ml (½pint) double cream
8 egg yolks

25 g (1oz) sultanas
175 g (6oz) caster sugar
25 g (1oz) raisins
1 vanilla pod or a few drops of vanilla essence
To Finish —caster sugar

Method

Grease a 1.75ltr (3 pint) pudding basin with butter.
First, butter the bread, remove the crusts and cut in half diagonally, creating triangles. Whisk the egg yolks and caster sugar together in a bowl. Split the vanilla pod, if using, and place in a pan with the milk and cream or add the vanilla essence. Bring the milk and cream to the simmer, then sieve onto the egg yolks, stirring all the time. You now have the custard.
Arrange the bread in layers in the prepared basin, sprinkling the sultanas and raisins in between layers. Finish with a final layer of bread without any fruit on top as this tends to burn. The warm egg mixture may now be poured over the bread and cooked straightaway, but I prefer to pour the custard over the pudding then leave it to soak into the bread for 20 minutes before cooking. This allows the bread to take on a new texture and have the flavours all the way through. Pre-heat the oven to 180°C/350°F/gas mark 4.
Once the bread has been soaked, place the dish in a roasting tray three-quarters filled with warm water. Lightly cover with buttered foil and place in the pre-heated oven. Cook for about 20-30 minutes until the pudding begins to set. Because we are using only egg yolks, the mixture cooks like a fresh custard and only thickens; it should not become too firm.
When ready, remove from the water bath, sprinkle liberally with caster sugar to cover, and glaze under the grill on medium heat. The sugar will dissolve and caramelize and you may find that the corners of the bread start to burn a little. This helps the flavours, though, giving a bittersweet taste, and certainly looks good. The bread and butter pudding is now ready to serve and when you take that first spoonful and place it in a bowl you will see the custard just seeping from the dish. You now have a new British classic at its best.
Note: Freshly grated or ground nutmeg can be sprinkled between the layers for an extra spicy flavour.

Gary Rhodes — Chef

CARAMELISED APPLE TART TATIN

Ingredients

60g butter, softened - unsalted
100g castor sugar
100g acacia honey
6 granny smith apples
6 star anise
3 vanilla pods, halved
750g puff pastry

6 x 250ml ramekins
You can make this recipe with most fruits.
For soft fruit, such as strawberry and banana, roll the pastry thinner (about 1½mm) and cook for shorter time, about 15 minutes.

Method

Preheat the oven to 200°C/400°F/gas mark 6 and put a baking sheet in the oven to heat. Use the butter to heavily grease 6 x 250ml ramekins.
Put the sugar and honey in a small pan and heat gently, stirring until the sugar has dissolved. Bring to a simmer and boil for 5 minutes, without stirring, or until you have a rich golden-brown caramel. Pour the caramel in to the bases of the ramekins.
Peel and core the apples — then take a slice approximately 1cm from the top and the bottom of each. Place one apple in each ramekin, making sure the tops of the apples are level with the tops of the ramekins. Put one star anise and half a vanilla pod in the hollow centre of each apple. Place on to the preheated baking sheet and bake for 15 minutes or until just tender.
Meanwhile, roll out the pastry disc over each baked apple, tucking the edges of the pastry down the sides of the apple, and return to the oven for 18-20 minutes until the pastry is crisp and golden. Leave to cool slightly, then invert on to the serving plates.
Serve with scoop of vanilla or caramel ice-cream.

Jean Christophe Novelli — Chef

CHAIRMAN'S PUDDING

Ingredients

1 pint milk (full fat or semi-skimmed)
1 pint whipping cream
26g (1oz) caster sugar
4 egg yolks (size 2)
2 eggs (size 2)
100g (3½oz) sultanas
70g (2½oz) butter
small loaf of white bread, medium sliced (approx 16 slices)

Method

Pour the milk and cream into a pan and bring to the boil. Whisk egg yolks, eggs and caster sugar. Then add hot milk and cream mixture and blend. Strain into a bowl.

Sprinkle half the sultanas into the bottom of a medium-sized ovenproof dish. Remove crusts from bread slices and cut into diagonal quarters. Arrange diagonal quarters in the dish, overlapping each layer until the dish is filled, placing small cubes of butter on the bread. Pour egg mix over the bread and sprinkle with remaining sultanas.

Place in a deep baking tin, half filled with warm water. Cook in the oven at 150°C/300°F/gas mark 2 for approx 50 minutes or until golden brown.

Rasberry sauce: Puree and sieve 200g (7oz) fresh raspberries. Bring to the boil 75g (3oz) sugar and 75ml (2½fl oz) red burgundy with a slice of lemon rind. Add raspberry puree and reduce for about 3-4 minutes.

Apricot sauce: Blanch, skin and stone 250g (9oz) of ripe apricots. Puree in a blender with 7tbsp of sugar syrup (boil equal amounts of water and sugar for 3-4 minutes). Stir in 2 tsp of fresh lime juice.

These sauces can be served warm or cold.

When serving, pour the raspberry sauce on to the plate, surround it with the apricot sauce and place a portion of pudding on top. If you are intent on going entirely over the top, a scoop of frozen yoghurt on the side will certainly do the trick.

Mohammed Al Fayed — Chairman of Harrods

FRENCH APPLE PUDDING

"I'm not a great pudding person but this marriage of sweet, sharp and alcohol is persuasive!"

Ingredients

3 large apples
2 tbsp sugar
dash fresh lemon juice
2 tbsp butter
cinnamon and sifted vanilla sugar

5fl oz milk
2-3 eggs
3½oz flour
1tbsp sugar
A generous splash of Calvados (or rum)

Method

Pre-heat oven to 180˚C/350°F/gas mark 4

Peel, core and slice the apples. Sprinkle them with the 2 tbsp of sugar, lemon juice and a little cinnamon. Cover and leave to stand for about half an hour. During that time turn the slices over occasionally so they are well impregnated with the lemon juice, sugar and cinnamon.
Make a batter with the milk, eggs and flour, 1tbsp of sugar and calvados (or rum , in which case you will have to call this West Indian Apple Pudding!)
Melt the butter in a deep gratin dish.
Mix the apples with the batter and pour onto the hot butter. Bake at gas mark 4 until top is firm. Then turn the whole thing over – pancake style. Don't fret if it breaks! When the top is brown tear the pudding into smaller pieces (this is easiest with two forks). Return the dish to the oven until the smaller pieces are lightly browned but still a little moist inside.
Serve in the gratin dish dusted thickly with sifted vanilla sugar and cinnamon.

Pat St Clement — Actress

GOLDEN SYRUP SPONGE

Ingredients

3oz sugar
2 eggs
4oz flour
2oz butter
1 tsp baking powder

Method

Cream butter and sugar, add eggs and flour and baking powder, add a very small quantity of hot water if the mixture is too stiff. Pour into well greased and floured individual moulds or a basin and cover with greaseproof paper and foil and steam or boil for 1½ hours at least.

Serve with warmed golden syrup and custard or cream.

Bernard Cribbins — Actror

SPONGE CAKE AND CHOCOLATE CUSTARD

Ingredients

Per pint of liquid include:
2oz soft margarine
2oz caster sugar
2oz self-raising flour (sieved)
1 egg
splash of milk

Custard
1 tbsp custard powder (heaped)
1 tsbp cornflour
1 tbsp of cocoa powder
1 tbsp soft brown sugar
250ml (9fl oz) milk

In order to make a chocolate sponge cake (which, of course, is the best kind) replace some of the flour with sieved cocoa powder.

Method

Cream the margarine and sugar together, gradually add the flour, cocoa and eggs, making sure that the ingredients are blended to a uniform consistency. Add the splash of milk, and mix well.
Baking times will vary, depending on how big the cake is, but the oven should be at 160°C/320°F/gas mark 3.

For the custard:
Mix the custard powder, cornflour, sugar and milk together and pour into a saucepan. Slowly heat the liquid until almost to the boil, stirring constantly, so that the mixture thickens to a custard.
Take off the heat and add the cream and chocolate sauce. Stir until the chocolate sauce has blended into the custard and serve.

"I fell in love with this in school and have loved it ever since!"

Adrian Dickson — Presenter

ROLY POLY

Ingredients

225g flour
pinch of salt
30ml castor sugar
10ml baking powder
75g shredded suet
150ml water
225g sultanas
15ml milk

Method

Sift flour, salt, sugar and baking powder into bowl. Stir in suet. Gradually add water to form a dough.
Roll out to rectangle about ¼in thick. Sprinkle sultanas over dough. Brush edges with milk and roll up like a swiss roll — seal edges.
Enclose the roly poly in foil, leaving room for expansion. Put into a large pan half filled with hot water and steam over low heat for 2½ hours.

"A real treat after cycling round Balamory!"

PC Plum —Balamory PC

STICKY TOFFEE PUDDING

Ingredients

55g/2oz butter
170g/6oz demerara sugar
2 tbsp black treacle
1 tbsp golden syrup
2 eggs
200g/7oz self-raising flour
200g/7oz pitted dates
290ml/10fl oz boiling water
1 tbsp bicarbonate of soda
1 tsp vanilla extract

For the sauce:
110ml/4fl oz double cream
55g/2oz butter, diced
55g/2oz dark muscovado sugar
2 tbsp black treacle
1 tbsp golden syrup

For the moulds:
30g/1oz soft butter
30g/1oz flour

Method

Butter the moulds and dust with flour and preheat oven to 200˚C/400˚F/gas mark 6.

Using a food processor, cream the butter and sugar together. Slowly add the golden syrup, treacle and eggs. Continue mixing until the mixture looks smooth, then turn down to a slow speed and add the flour. Mix until everything is well combined.

Add the boiling water to the dates and tip into a blender. Secure the lid firmly and blend to a puree. Add the bicarbonate of soda and vanilla. Pour this into the batter while it is still hot and stir well.

Pour into the moulds and bake for 20-25 minutes until the tops are just firm to the touch.

Make the sauce:

simply place all the ingredients in a pan, bring to the boil, stirring a few times and then remove from the heat. Put to one side until ready to use.

Remove the puddings from the moulds and place on plate. Coat with the warmed sauce and serve with good vanilla ice cream.

© James Martin

Chris Tarrant — Presenter

PLUM DUFF

Ingredients

3 handfuls self-raising flour
½ loaf of crumbs
1 packet shredded suet
3 boxes mixed spice
1 tsp baking powder
5 eggs and a little milk (don't make it too moist)
¾lb sugar
3lb plums

Method

Mix together ingredients. Make into a round ball.
Put in a clean white cloth, tie tight.
Put into a large pot of boiling water and cook for about 3 hours.

Best Wishes
Jim Cricket

Jimmy Cricket — Entertainer

QUEEN OF PUDDINGS WITH BANANA CUSTARD

"The banana custard really lifts the flavour of this great old English pudding."

Ingredients

300ml (½ pint) milk
150ml (¼ pint) double cream
½ tsp vanilla essence
1 small lemon
100g (4oz) fresh white breadcrumbs
25g (1oz) unsalted butter

75g (3oz) castor sugar
4-6 tbsp raspberry jam
2 eggs
150g (5oz) natural yogurt
2 tsp clear honey
2 small bananas

Method

Put the milk, cream and vanilla essence in a saucepan and bring to the boil. Grate in the lemon rind then stir in the breadcrumbs, butter and 25g (1oz) of the sugar. Cook over a low heat for 2-3 minutes, stirring. Pour into a 900ml (1¼ pint) ovenproof dish and leave for about 5 minutes to allow a skin to form.

Pre-heat the oven to 220°C/450°F/ gas mark 8.

Put the jam in a small pan over a low heat, until melted.

Separate the eggs. Whisk the egg whites in a large bowl until stiff, then quickly whisk in the remaining sugar. Spoon into a piping bag fitted with a large star nozzle.

Sieve the jam over the surface of the pudding, then pipe the meringue mixture on top. Place in the oven and bake for about 5 minutes until the meringue is golden.

Meanwhile, make the custard. Put the egg yolks in a small pan with the yogurt and honey and place over a low heat. Cut the bananas into thin slices and add to the pan.

Cook until the mixture boils and thickens, stirring constantly,

Serve the pudding hot, with plenty of custard.

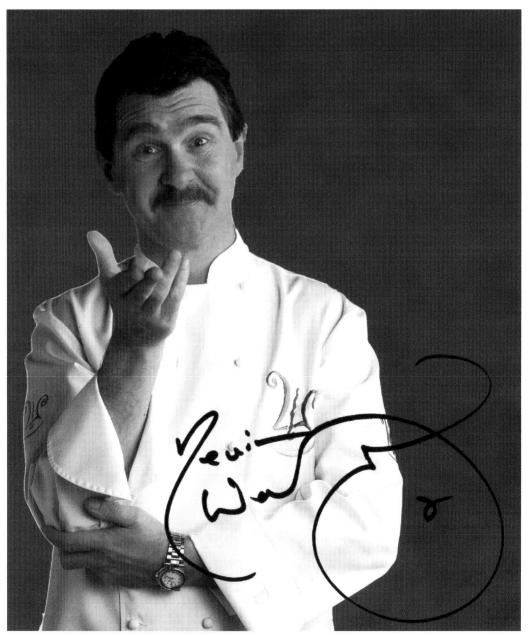

Kevin Woodford — Chef
© Juliet Piddington

STICKY TOFFEE PUDDING

Ingredients

6oz pitted dates
1 tsp bicarbonate of soda
½ pint of water
2oz butter
6g castor sugar
2 eggs
6oz self raising flour
1lb butter
1lb brown sugar
1 pint whipping cream

Method

Simmer chopped dates, then add bicarbonate of soda.
Cream butter and sugar, add beaten eggs, and fold in flour. Stir in date mixture.
Put in a square pan and bake in oven at 190°C/375°F/gas mark 5 for 20–25 minutes.

To make the sauce, melt butter, add sugar and cream and bring to a slow boil. Serve warm, spooned over pudding.

"Yum yum."

Hayley Mills — Actress

GRAPE SPECIAL

"This is a recipe that I and my family particularly enjoy. It is simple, but delicious."

Ingredients

1lb seedless grapes (if unavailable, de-pipping is essential)
large block vanilla ice cream
soft brown sugar
½ pint double cream

Method

Put grapes into a fireproof dish, cover with the cream, and put into fridge overnight.
About 10 or 12 minutes before the dish is required, heat grill. Cover the grapes with thick slices of ice cream, then cover ice cream with at least ¼" brown sugar, making sure no ice cream is showing through. Put under a very hot grill until the surface of the sugar is sizzling. A few seconds after removing from the grill, the sugar will cool and form a toffee apple-type surface over the whole dish.

Ronnie Barker
Comedian

Baking

ALL-IN-ONE CHOCOLATE SPONGE

Ingredients

110g self-raising flour (sifted)
1 tsp baking powder
110g soft margarine, at room temperature
110g caster sugar
2 large eggs
1 tbsp cocoa powder
icing sugar, jam and/or fresh cream

Method

Pre-heat the oven to 170°C/325°F/gas mark 3.

You will need two 18cm sponge tins, no less than 4cm deep, lightly greased and lined with greaseproof paper (also greased) or silicone paper.

Take a large roomy mixing bowl and sift flour and baking powder into it, holding the sieve high to give the flour a good airing. Then simply add all the other ingredients to the bowl, and whisk them, preferably with an electric hand whisk, till thoroughly combined. If the mixture doesn't drop off a wooden spoon easily when tapped on the side of the bowl, then add 1 or 2 tsp of tap warm water, and whisk again.

Now divide the mixture between the two prepared tins, level off and bake on the centre shelf of the oven for about 30 minutes. When cooked leave them in the tins for only about 30 seconds, then loosen the edges by sliding a palette knife all round and turn them out onto a wire cooling rack. Peel off the base papers carefully and, when cool, sandwich them together with jam or lemon curd (or jam and fresh cream), and dust with icing sugar.

Tony Blair — Prime Ministe

CHOCOLATE BROWNIES

Ingredients

375g soft unsalted butter
375g best-quality dark chocolate
6 large eggs
1 tbsp vanilla extract
500g castor sugar
225g plain flour
1 tsp salt
50g white chocolate (roughly chopped)

Method

Preheat oven to 180°C /350°F/gas mark 4. Line your brownie pan — I think it's worth lining the sides as well as the base — with foil, parchment or Bake-O-Glide.

Melt the butter and chocolate together in a large heavy-based pan. In a bowl or large wide-mouthed measuring jug, beat the eggs with the sugar and vanilla. Measure the flour into another bowl and add the salt.

When the chocolate mixture is melted, let it cool a bit before beating in the eggs and sugar, and then the white chocolate and flour. Beat to combine smoothly and then scrape out of the saucepan into the lined pan.

Bake for about 25 minutes. When it's ready, the top should be dried to a paler brown speckle, but the middle still dark and dense and gooey. And even with such a big batch, you need to keep alert, keep checking: the difference between gungy brownies and dry brownies is only a few minutes; remember that they will continue to cook as they cool.

Trinny Woodall
What Not To Wear
BBC TV

© adapted from a recipe by Nigella Lawson

CIDER CAKE

"From Clarrie and Eddie Grundy - at least Eddie's scrumpy comes in useful for something!"

Ingredients

4oz butter
4oz sugar
2 beaten eggs
8oz sifted self raising flour
1 tsp bicarbonate of soda
½ tsp grated nutmeg
7fl oz cider
caster sugar for sprinkling

Method

Cream the butter and sugar. Beat in the eggs. Fold in half of the flour, bicarbonate and nutmeg. Pour in the cider and mix. Fold in the remaining flour. Bake in a shallow, greased tin (8" by 5") at 180°C/350°F, gas mark 4, for 35 -40 minutes. When cool cut into squares and sprinkle with caster sugar.

"Delicious with a glass of cider!"

Eddie & Clarrie Grundy
The Archers
BBC Radio 4

BISCUIT CAKE

Ingredients

½lb Rich Tea biscuits
4oz butter
1½oz cocoa powder
1½ heaped tbsp syrup
4oz plain (Bourneville) chocolate

Method

Bash biscuits.
Melt butter, syrup and cocoa powder then mix together with the crushed biscuits.
Grease tin with butter and put mixture in.
Flatten down and leave in fridge.
Melt chocolate in a bowl over hot water.
Pour over the biscuit mixture and return to fridge.
When set turn out and cut into squares.

"Delicious on picnics or to nibble in the daisy bus!"

Edie McCedie — Actress

CARROT CAKE

Ingredients

2 cups plain flour
2 cups sugar
4 eggs
2oz butter
2 cups grated carrots
1 cup raisins
1 cup walnuts
1 tsp cinnamon
1 tsp ginger
nutmeg
vanilla essence
2 tsp baking powder

Method

Mix butter and sugar until creamy. Add one egg with a little flour.
Then add carrots in mixing bowl and other ingredients

Bake for 40 mins. 180°C/350°F/gas mark 4

You can also apply this for Banana Cake.

Michael Caine — Actor

CHOCOLATE RUM CAKE

Ingredients

5oz plain flour
1oz cocoa powder
1 tsp salt
2 tsp baking powder
5oz soft brown sugar
2 eggs
6 tbsp corn/veg. oil
6 tbsp milk
½ tsp vanilla essence

For the rum syrup:
4oz granulated sugar
¼ pint water
2 tbsp rum

For the decoration:
6fl oz double cream
grated plain chocolate.

Method

Sift the flour, salt, cocoa powder, and baking powder into a large mixing bowl. Add soft brown sugar. Separate the eggs, cracking the yolks into a small basin and the whites into a larger one. Add the corn oil, milk and vanilla essence to the yolks and mix with a fork. Pour into the centre of the dry ingredients and using a wooden spoon mix well to make a smooth batter. Whisk the egg whites until stiff and fold into the mixture. Pour the cake mixture into a greased and lined tin 8½" by 1½". Heat the oven to 180°C/350°F/gas mark 4 and bake for 40 to 45 minutes. Turn out and allow to cool.

Meanwhile measure the sugar and water for the syrup into a saucepan and stir over a low heat until the sugar dissolves. Bring to the boil and simmer for 5 minutes to concentrate the syrup. Draw off the heat and stir in the rum. Replace the cake in the original baking tin, prick holes over the surface with a skewer and pour over the hot syrup. Leave to soak over night.

To serve turn the cake out on a serving plate; whisk the cream until thick and swirl over top and sides. Decorate with grated chocolate curls and chill for several hours before serving.

Richard Griffiths — Actor

FAVOURITE CHOCOLATE GATEAU

Ingredients

3 eggs (size 2 or 3)
4oz sugar
grated rind and juice of 1 lemon
2oz plain flour
1oz each cornflour and cocoa
4oz butter or margarine

For filling:
1 pint double or whipping cream
small quantity of fruit in syrup
(e.g. pitted cherries)

For syrup:
½ pint water
1lb sugar
grated rind of half an orange and
half a lemon
½ cinnamon stick
1 or 2 cloves
orange flavoured liqueur to taste

For decoration:
¼lb plain chocolate

Method

To make cake, whisk eggs, sugar and lemon rind and juice together over bowl of warm water until light-coloured and thick enough to hold shape. Sift dry ingredients and fold in gently. Melt butter or margarine over low heat and pour into mixture (without sediment). Mix well. Place in greased round tin 8-9" and bake 20/25 minutes in moderate oven 375°F/190°C/gas mark 4/5. Turn out of tin before fully cooled. When cold, cut cake into four thin layers.

For syrup heat water and sugar gently until sugar is dissolved, then boil with orange and lemon juice and spices until mixture is thick. Cool, remove spices, then add liqueur to taste.

Whisk cream until thick and fold in the fruit together with some of the fruit syrup. Spread the bottom layer of cake with syrup and cover with some of the cream filling. Repeat with other layers and spread remaining cream on top of cake.

Make chocolate curls by scraping knife blade across chocolate and use to decorate cake as desired.

Cleo Laine — Singer

GIGGLE CAKE

Ingredients

2 tsp melted butter, for greasing
12oz mixed dried fruit
4¼oz butter or margarine
6oz soft brown sugar
8oz self-raising flour
pinch of salt
2 eggs, beaten
8oz canned, chopped pineapple, drained
4¼oz glace cherries, halved

Method

Put the mixed dried fruit into a large bowl and cover with boiling water. Set aside to soak for 10-15 minutes, then drain well. Put the butter or margarine and sugar into a large saucepan and heat gently until melted.

Add the drained dried fruit and cook over a low heat, stirring frequently, for 4-5 minutes. Remove from the heat and transfer to a mixing bowl, set aside to cool.

Sift the flour and salt into the dried fruit mixture and stir well. Add the eggs, mixing until the ingredients are thoroughly blended together.

Add the pineapple and cherries to the cake mixture and stir to combine. Transfer to a greased and lined 1lb loaf tin and level the surface. Bake in a pre-heated oven at 180°C/350°F/gas mark 4 for about an hour. Test with a fine skewer, if it comes out clean it is cooked, if not return to the oven for a few more minutes.

Remove from the oven and allow to cool before serving.

Midge Ure — Musican

TRUFFLE TORT

Ingredients

100g unsalted butter,softened
100g caster sugar
3 eggs, separated, whites stiffly beaten
100g plain chocolate, melted
25g plain flour
150g ground hazelnuts

Chocolate icing
150 ml double cream
150g plain chocolate/broken into pieces
8 chocolate spirals

Method

Butter and line an 18cm/7" spring-form cake tin with greaseproof paper. Brush the paper with melted butter and dust with flour.

Beat the butter in a mixing bowl, until pale and soft. Add the sugar and beat until light and fluffy. Add the egg yolks, one at a time, beating well after each addition. Stir in the melted chocolate. Sift together the flour and hazelnuts and then sift again into the mixing bowl. Fold into the butter mixture. Gently fold in a third of the beaten egg whites, then fold in the rest.

Pour the mixture into the prepared tin and bake in a preheated oven for 55-60 minutes or until firm and springy to the touch.

Remove from the oven and leave the cake in the tin on a wire tray for 5 minutes before turning it out to cool completely.

To make the icing, place the cream in a saucepan and bring just to the boil. Add the chocolate, stirring until the chocolate melts and the mixture is thick and smooth. Pour the mixture evenly over the cake; before the chocolate sets, decorate with 8 chocolate spirals.

Lesley Joseph — Actresss

VICTORIA SPONGE

Ingredients

6oz wholemeal, self-raising flour
6oz softened butter
6oz caster sugar
3 eggs, beaten
1-2 tbsp water
3 tbsp raspberry jam
icing sugar to dredge

Method

Pre-heat oven to 180°C/350°F/gas mark 4.
Grease and line two 18cm (7") tins (which you won't be able to find).
Do what you have to do to make the butter and sugar into a fluffy mixture — I put it in a food processor myself, but then I'm very rich.
Gradually add eggs, beating mixture as you go. Fold in the flour (sift it first if you can be fagged).
Divide the mixture between the 2 tins, smoothe tops and put into oven for 25/30 minutes. (If you have an Aga, they will burn shortly.) To test if ready, press lightly and they should spring back. (If they're burnt, you'll spring back.) Cool on a rack, then stick them together with jam and cover with icing sugar.

"Once cake is ready, put it in a rusty cake tin and forget about it."

Victoria Wood — Comedienne

BEDS GARDEN CARERS

Reg Charity No. 1091271

BGC was set up by Bedford Mencap in April 1997 as a garden maintenance project to provide hands-on work experience for adults with learning disabilities. As well as the Garden Force, we now have a furniture workshop and can offer a variety of Educational experiences. Our first adults joined us in May 1997.

"We want to be like you, do the things you do and take for granted. Independent living for us is still having somebody to help us with such things as paying bills, doing the shopping, housework and reading letters. We are trying but some of us will never get there on our own. We want to go out to work like you, but for most of us this will never happen. Some of us can read and write, not all, most of us will never drive a car, some of us are on medication we will need to have for the rest of our lives. We want to have intimate relationships, maybe have children, but very few of us will. We live next door to you but in a different world. We have been hidden in institutions for decades and now want to be part of your society, just like you.
We would not be able to do half the things we do at the moment if it was not for projects such as BGC."

Thank you for buying this book,

Brian Alexander
Steven Bolger
Mark Bradford
Tim Branson
Steven Brill
Dennis Butt
Ian Cooper
Erica Creer
Robert Hill
Stuart Goldsmith
Lisa Lowing &
Rosaleen Murphy

BGC
Kingsway House
13 Kingsway
Bedford
MK42 9BJ
Tel: 01234 352899
Fax: 01234 357981
Email: sharon@bedsgardencarers.org.uk
www.bedsgardencarers.org.uk

INVESTOR IN PEOPLE